Behind the Eyes
of a
Shadow Girl

Behind the Eyes
of a
Shadow Girl

M. R. Faith

authorHOUSE®

AuthorHouse™
1663 Liberty Drive
Bloomington, IN 47403
www.authorhouse.com
Phone: 1 (800) 839-8640

Published by AuthorHouse   09/09/2015

ISBN: 978-1-5049-4887-6 (sc)
ISBN: 978-1-5049-4886-9 (e)

Library of Congress Control Number: 2015914704

Print information available on the last page.

Contents

Behind the eyes of a shadow girl is dedicated to my children Krista, Caitlyn, and Dominic, you are what kept me going in the darkness and helped bring me to the light. I love you all the way to heaven and back.

Chapter 1

ESTABLISHING MY PATH

From the time I was in my mom's tummy my granny knew I was going to be a very special person, a leader, a healer, and a helper to those in the world of the Christians. Granny absolutely loved me with all her heart. She never judged me for anything I said or did. I stayed at Granny's house all the time as I was growing up, it was my second home. We did things together, talked about everything and never hid anything from each other. Our favorite thing to do together was watch the Houston Astros playing live on television or listen to them on the radio. Granny absolutely adored baseball and so did I.

She was the most real, down to earth, Christian woman I have ever known. She was caring, loving, she had compassion for others, understanding, and never judged anyone but at the same time she was hard core and wasn't scared of anything. When kids now a day's get in trouble they get their electronics and cell phones taken away. But when we were kids at Granny's, she did not play a round. When we acted up at her house she would give us a warning then finally tell us to go outside and pick a branch from the tree in the middle of her yard. If it wasn't sufficient she would go outside herself and pick a bigger branch that had knots all over it. She would explain to us why we were in trouble and then the spanking commenced. She got our butts, arms, and legs. It didn't matter if we ran. She'd swing that switch at us then whack us harder... I tell you what though for her to spank us meant we were really being little heathens.

One weekend when I was about 5 years old, granny had me over for the night. We were hanging out in the living room, granny sitting in her favorite rocking chair, knitting and I was on the couch next to her eating vanilla ice cream with crushed up cookies and m & m's. Lord have mercy! No wonder I was a fat little kid. There was a commercial on about Jesus. So granny asked me "do know who Jesus is?" I said, without blinking an eye, yes, of course I know who Jesus is. He is my brother and friend and God is our father. She seemed amazed so then she asked me if I knew what the bible was? I said yes again. I said "Granny, you know what? God has given me a gift to share with you. Do you want to know what it is?" She said "Tell me." Now ladies and gentlemen keep in mind that I was not one of the smartest kids by far, and I always had trouble learning in school and never could really grasp it all. Actually at 5 I couldn't even really read yet because I was behind for my age.

I explained to her that I've had these feelings of people around me, like when I would look at some of them I would see a light around them because they were one of God's children. Then I would look at some of them and I would see pure evil in them and that was the devil. I also told her at night when she prayed and read the bible that angels were standing around her.

"The last thing is that I know God's Word granny and he told me to tell you some of it". Then I began to quote scripture to her. The first thing I said was "For I know the plans I have for you," declares the LORD, "plans to prosper you and not harm you, plans to give you hope and a future. Jeremiah 29: 11. Boy I tell you what I never saw my granny move so fast. She jumped up and ran across the living room and flipped open the bible to that passage I quoted. She was floored. She said, "ok, little lady, can you tell me another passage? Thinking maybe that I had heard that one from someone in the family, I said sure and told her "Out of the mouths of babes and infants you have established strength because of your foes, to still the enemy and avenger." Psalms 8: 2. She sat down right where she was standing. She could not believe her own ears. She knew in her heart I was meant to do great things in life and the world but she never thought it was that anointed. I said "Granny all of us children have an idea about what we want to do when we grow up, like, I love fishing with my dad so I want to work with sea animals but that doesn't mean that is what my path is supposed to be."

"God has a plan for each and every one of us so you can choose to follow the path he gives you or go down your own path. Granny, he gave us free will to be able to make decisions on our own, but no matter what path you choose God will always set you straight in time. HE says that to trust in the LORD with all your heart and do not lean on your own understanding. In all ways acknowledge Him and He will make your paths. Proverbs 3:5-6." Then I told her I knew all of this because God gave it to me as a gift to share with her.

God gave me a gift to lead my family to heavens gates and many other people in the world. We talked on about everything for hours and I will never forget that day. I've have always felt this connection with her and told her everything that I would not dare tell anyone else. The things I felt the things I saw and the things I did. I didn't share anything with another soul, not anyone else in my family or school like I did with her. I felt unloved, shunned, unwanted, & different from everyone else. The only one who truly listened to me and talked to me was granny. She truly believed in me and the things I spoke with her about and she never told anyone else what we talked about. Well, as far as I know of, because I was already having problems with life and my surroundings and she knew I didn't want anyone else to judge me more than they already did. I carried a lot of weight on my shoulders at a very young age, and as I grew I had no idea what my life was going to be like. When you're a small child you see things differently. You still have wants, dreams, inspirations and desires. That innocence is still there and you feel a range of emotions but it's different from the emotions of an adult. A child's innocence is a very precious gift that should be held onto as long as possible.

Chapter 2

BEHIND THE EYES
OF A CHILD

I didn't feel like a normal child. I saw life differently. I saw life around me, actual life, with a meaning. I saw the plants, the trees, the animals and even the spiders and that they were alive. It was very intriguing to just sit and watch the wind blow through the trees and listen to the sounds of the earth and the animals speaking. It was all just very soothing to me, more soothing than listening to my parents fighting and screaming at each other as I hid in the other room. Being outside relaxed me and made me feel at peace inside. I would sit on my front porch and sing to the ants and they would look at me and dance around as they went about their business I just saw it for what it was, God's creation.

Now back to the fighting thing. I was not from your typical good home. My parents fought constantly. They did not like one another. They yelled and screamed at me and my brother all of the time. There was a dark cloud of oppression over our home and every time you entered you could feel the tension in the air, the unhappiness, the broken heartedness and the fear of what was going to happen next. My parents were not happy and they tended to take it out on my brother and me. It's like we had to walk on egg shells around the house.

Now I know everyone got pops as a kid back when I was young. There were no time outs or taking away toys or electronics. It was bend over and be prepared to feel the burn! My mom would try to discipline us but it never worked. We knew our way around her so she would yell and scream then finally make us sit in the kitchen chairs in the living room till dad got home. By the time dad got home he was tired of hearing mom yell at him for what we did so he would not just pop our little behinds. He would beat us. By the time he was done with us we would have welts from the belt on our butt's and legs or wherever it got us if we did not hold still. He would talk down to us and tell us how pathetic and stupid we were and that we were a worthless bunch of kids. I knew that this came from the rage and anger he had built up inside. I know my dad loved us and afterwards he would feel bad about what happened so he always tried to make up for it by taking us on trips camping or whatever for instance

Garner state park or New Braunfels with his friends. I absolutely loved camping and being outdoors. I was a bit of a tomboy growing up plus I just love being outside around the mountains the trees the grass the river. It is all just so very fascinating to me. And when I was outside I could hear everything. The sound of the world is so amazing when you actually stop and listen. It really made me appreciate the world and the life in it. It was the only time as a child I felt at peace.

Then when I was about six I saw my first scary people. My room was upstairs then so mom had put me to bed and I couldn't sleep. I would just lay there and listen to my parents fight and stare at the clown I had made in school that was hanging on my closet door. The closet door was closed. All the lights were off but I felt like something was in the room watching me. Then I heard shuffling in the closet. Of course I was scared of the dark and I wasn't going to open that door. Matter fact I would jump off my bed across the room to reach the light switch just to turn the light on at night so I could go to the restroom because the thing that lived under my bed and pulled on my feet at night was not going to get me. I heard the closest door begin to open. I laid there really still and pulled the covers up to my eyes like it wouldn't know I was there...

Then a tall man and a tall skinny lady with hair past her butt came walking towards me with their arms held out in front of them. I don't know how I got to the door and downstairs but I did. I ran around screaming with my dad running behind me and my mom behind him with the broom for a good 10 minutes before they caught up to me. Needless to say they made me go back upstairs and investigate and found nothing but the closet door open. They said I made it up. I didn't ever sleep in that room again and eventually switched rooms later to the room down stairs that was the study and it became my permanent residence for years. I now believe the people and things that were under my bed when I was a child were my first interactions with demons... Yes America, I said demons.

My family was an unusual group of people. We had our Christians, hippies, witches and ghost chasers. When I was about 8 years old my mom took me over to my grandma's house and there was my two cousins sitting on the floor playing the Ouija board and my me maw sitting in her chair watching. They told us to hurry up and come in and sit down. Now me maws house was behind a huge graveyard and there was always activity going on over there. I tell you what. I was one scared little white girl but it fascinated me. So we're sitting there on the couch watching my cousins play on the Ouija board and my mom and I just arrived and they were talking to one of my cousins' friends on the board. It was a ghost boy. I didn't know what to expect so I sat there quietly, with my eyes wide open, watching, right next to my mom. It started moving and they got all excited. He tells my one cousin something which I really don't know what it was because I didn't see the board but she did not like it and she told the boy to leave her alone and never come back.

Next thing you know the Ouija board hovers up and goes flying across the living room. Everyone started screaming and flipping on lights and running around and I jumped up and yelled, "Satan leave this house and leave my family alone!" I don't know for sure why I did that but I think it was that little boy and he was really not a boy he was a demon trying to get hold of my cousin.

But back then I did not realize what a demon was. Back then I thought it was just a little ghost boy playing tricks on us. That night changed my reality and the way I saw the world for the rest of my young life. I felt compelled to fight the bad thing that happened that night and what I was feeling. I wanted to learn more about all of what was going on and I wanted them ghost boys or whatever it may have been to know I was fearless and I was going to kick their butts! I knew I had God on my side and they couldn't touch me but boy was I wrong. Now they couldn't physically touch me I knew but they could do other things to me. They will and can destroy you in any way possible.

From birth God had a plan for me and the devil knew it. Everything seemed fine so far in life. Normal stuff you know, well what I thought was normal. Until when I was 10, my brother and I were at my granny's house, and my dad showed up, sat down and told us that my mom and he were getting a divorce. My heart sank into my stomach and my eyes filled with tears. My family had now been torn apart. My world was coming down and crashing on top of me. I didn't understand why my parents did not want to be together or if it was something I had done or my brother. All I knew was I was no longer going to be able to see both my parents at night and have dinner together and do things together no more and prayers and hugs and love from both of them. It was hard to understand and it killed me inside. It broke me totally apart.

I had never felt any kind of pain like that in my young life. It was devastating news and I felt as if someone died. My emotions were all over the place and I wasn't sure how to handle this. About that point is when the negativity took place in my life. Neither of my parents had one good thing to say about the other and all they cared about was money. It was consuming them. They didn't have one thing to say nor do with us kids unless they had to so we stayed at home by ourselves night after night or at her granny's house. From there on out it's like they totally just forgot about my brother and I. It was like a tornado cutting through our lives. I began to become a rebel, didn't do what I was supposed to, but wouldn't want my brother to. I acted out at school. I didn't do my chores. I didn't want anything to do with anybody. I sheltered myself and withdrew from society and life. I didn't care about anything. I was miserable, depressed, oppressed and couldn't stand the thought of anything but my granny. Granny always found a way to make things better somehow but at home I just went through the motions. I watched television, played Nintendo, went outside and played with the neighbors kids, ate and went to bed. I had begun to feel the numb inside especially the feelings I had with God we're slipping away from me.

Then both parents remarried and had their own lives now, while my brother and I had to adapt not knowing really what to think, feel or do. We were two different families with new step-siblings thrown into the mix of things who were probably just as confused as we were with their different backgrounds. Hmm step-siblings, I could write a whole other book on that subject. Let's just say blood is thicker than water no matter how close you are to a person. Living in a house with my dad, brother, step mom and her two sons was an experience in itself. Dad did try to make things fun and take us on trips and let us have friends over and just basically do what we wanted. Trying to keep us all under control and not having total chaos all the time was a chore in itself.

We all went skating every weekend and my brother and I were on the speed team and did competitions. I actually loved that part. My dad and step mom were big time dancers and dad taught dance class every week, and he was really good at it. Yet again all us kids were left unattended. Dad would go fishing and hunting. He also had his own business so he was just a really busy man. I know for a fact he loved us and cared for us. He just didn't have time for us. Then my mom's house was totally different. My step dad's son was grown and already out of the house, so it was just the two of them and us when we were there. It was always quiet. Mom worked and so did he. They did their own things at night and on the weekends too.

Chapter 3

WHEN DARKNESS FALLS

Over the next few years it was just kind of a fuzzy blur for the rest of my elementary school until 6th grade and it was a week before my 13th birthday. My life totally changed even worse than it had already been. Junior High year 6 grade and I was becoming a teen you would think leaving elementary school and going to junior high would be exciting for young lady and you think that it would be the prime time to enjoy your childhood out of elementary school finally starting to become a young adult almost in high school kids are excited about these kind of things. It's just something that should make you feel happy because you are at a new milestone in life but I wasn't happy about it at all. So one night I decided to sneak out and go to my friend's house. Her mom wasn't home and she had friends over hanging out. So I got there, and there was a bunch of people I didn't know and a lot of older guys. We hung out and talked. Some of them were drinking and carrying on with other things. It started getting really late so I decided I was going to go home. I told my friend bye and walked out the door and some guy came out afterwards I didn't know and said hey I can give you a ride home. I said I can walk. I only live a neighborhood over from here. He said, are you sure it's real late and I'm leaving anyways. Well not thinking it was a big deal I said ok and got in the Camaro with him.

This moment changed my life forever. It's something I will never forget ever, and I think about and will always remember till the day I die. We drove out of my friend's neighborhood then around to mine, but he didn't stop. He decided he wanted to go for a ride with me. This was the longest trip of my life, my stomach what in knots, I didn't know what was going on but I did not have a good feeling and was screaming inside filling up with panic. I was just freaking out, I sat in his car very still and calm because I was so scared. The guy pulled into the parking lot in order to get me in the backseat. I said no I'm not getting in the backseat I don't know why you're doing this but you can't make me. He said listen up little girl if you don't do what I say you won't make it home ever again. Tears were running down my face. I couldn't speak. I couldn't move. I was frozen. So he pulled me over into the backseat of his Camaro, held me down and started to pull down my pants. I snapped out of it and started screaming and kicking until he struck me in the face and started punching me over and over until he was able to take away that one thing I had left, my virginity.

I was still screaming and crying and this guy was mean and hitting me and telling me to stop or he would kill me, choking me, trying to make me stop. I didn't know what to think or do. All these thoughts were racing through my head. What if, what if, what if, what if I would've just walked home? Would this be happening? What if I'd just stayed home with my parents would this still be happening? Am I ever going to see my mom and dad again or my brother? Am I going to make it home or is he going to kill me after this? I thought he was going to rape me then kill me this horrible man was taking away my God given right to save my virginity that I had promised to keep until I was married one day. He took away the most precious thing from me that anyone could dare take. I was in so much pain, I was broken, my life had change drastically of this one decision, and my life would probably be over when ever this man was done with me so all I could do is lay there now.

I was in so much pain mentally and physically that I couldn't breathe, my air was gone, and I felt like my heart had stopped. I hurt all over from this grown man, man handling me for hours. I looked up at the stars and the moon and screamed for God to make him stop but he didn't. Did God even hear me? Why was he letting this happen to me? I was confused, I felt alone, abandoned and forgotten. If I die tonight no one will know what happened to me. My cries were not being heard by anyone not even God. I was just a shadow girl stuck in a dark world now with no one on my side or to care for me, and if I lived through this night I could never tell anyone about it. I could smell his cologne because it was strong and it smelled like lavender mixed in the air with my blood that he had beaten out of me over and over. I went limp finally because all of the fight I had was gone. All my hope left me; I surrendered to this ungodly man. This went on for many, many hours which felt like eternity, until the sun started to rise. I couldn't move. I just laid there and waited for it all to be over. I felt darkness all around me and deep within my soul. The enemy had won me over and that sweet little innocent girl was gone.

I had no idea what a long road was in front of me, that I began to walk after that night. I felt different now empty inside and disconnected. It was a week before my 13th birthday and my life had changed drastically. I couldn't even tell anyone about it because I was in fear for my life. I was battling demons at 12 years old that I should of never had to deal with. That man finally finished with me, he told me to put on my clothes and threw me a towel to wipe up the blood then took me home. I sat in the back seat all the way to my house. I couldn't move. He told me if I dare tell anyone that he would come back and take me again but next time he won't be taking me home. I said ok I won't say anything about it and I didn't not to anyone for many years.

I was battling demons at 12 years old I should have never had to deal with. Since I couldn't speak to anyone about my experience I began to lash out more. I started drinking, smoking weed, and cigarettes playing the Ouija board and doing spells trying to tap into the world beyond because my reality was a scary depressing unhappy place. I began to feel the demon that was attached to me. He was perched on my shoulders. He went with me everywhere. He whispered in my ears. He was in my mind and listening to all my thoughts. I thought my mind wasn't a holy, God filled and happy place anymore. It was a deep dark horrible place. I would lay awake at night and think about the darkness and the things that went bump in the night next to me didn't scare me anymore. They were now my friends; they were the ones I turn to when I could not turn to anything else or anyone else. I would lay there at night and talk to them, write poems about them. They were around me all of the time and I embraced them, I felt them perched on my shoulders and flying around me when I was out. This was my new darkness my new life was alone in the dark playing with demons.

My friends would all call and want me to sneak out and go do random things and go places with other random young people and do things I shouldn't be doing, like having sex, drinking and doing drugs. We would play with the dark side, tapping into whatever we could. We would go to graveyards, haunted houses, and anything else that we thought was crazy, we did. I saw bad and evil things. All the wonders of the world that made me happy were now gone. I was numb and all this darkness had taken over from the inside out. There was a hole in my chest now. I felt nothing. My heart beat still but it was filled with sadness and brokenness. I was a very gloomy sad, depressed, unhappy teenager and my path had been changed drastically. I had no supervision, no love, no cares, no guidance, no one to shake me and tell me that's enough stop what's wrong with you, nothing. I did what I wanted when I wanted, and I just continued that course of habit and chaos in my life by skipping, school hanging out with the wrong crowd, listening to loud crazy music, going out every night and partying with people I shouldn't even been around and having random meaningless flings with boys who I thought loved me but truly only wanted one thing from me.

By age 14 I had been beaten and raped 3 more times and blacked out and woke up in random places. My rapes were all different. Not one like the other but none of them was like the first either. The next one was at a party. I woke up from a dead sleep to a man on top off me. My pants we gone and he was holding me down and a gun being fired off above my head. It was a friend of mine who happened to have come back because he had forgotten something. That's the one I call the sneak attack, because he waited till I was drunk and passed out. The next one was at another party. This was a huge party at a house I had never been to. I went with an acquaintance. Kegs, liquor, and drugs you name it and it was there. So some guy kept feeding me beer and shots that tasted weird, on top of me doing 10 keg stands probably didn't help either. Anyways all I remember is him walking me to a dark room because I had thrown up and wanted to lie down. So I go to turn on the light but he wouldn't let me. I tried to scream so he covered my mouth and told me to lay down he had a surprise for me. I struggled with him for a few minutes then three other guys came into the room. They held me down and all had their way with me. I blacked out half way through it and woke up to an empty house like totally empty. That funny taste in my beer was most likely hard core pills to get me to pass out, and I did pass out! After that I tried to stay around my close friends and not venture off with new friends, but it happened again.

This time I was partying with my friends, but we had taken off to a party and were doing drugs and drinking. All I remember is meeting a girl and we were hanging out and having a good time. My friends wanted to leave so she said she would give me a ride home. Well that girl ended up letting her boyfriend beat and rape me, he choked me till I blacked out and woke up with blood everywhere. It looked like he had been putting items inside of me with the things that were on the ground by me, a hammer and some other tools, a ball, bungee cords which I think he tied my hands with, duct tape, candles, some other random items, and they all had blood on them. Who's ever house that was, there dad found me in the garage only because he heard me screaming. He calmed me down and helped me get up off the ground and into the house to help me clean up. I tried to explain what they looked like but he had no idea he said he had worked the night shift and his son takes advantage of it. So the nice man tried to talk me into calling the cops but I was terrified, so he took me home and I asked him to please not tell anyone. Matter of fact I didn't tell anyone about these incidents because I was so embarrassed...

The last time I was raped in my high school years was when I was staying with a new friend from the game room we all hung out at, and we were drinking a lot. Her parents were out of town, and her brothers and their friends were there. Well I think this was the last one anyways. She went to bed and I stayed up with one of the brothers friends drinking. I woke up the next morning butt naked on the couch covered up. I had bite marks and bruises all over me. The girl said she heard noises and came down and found him on top of me and I was passed out. She ran him out of the house, locked the doors and covered me up. So that would be the last time I spoke to her or anyone else that was there. To tell you the truth I don't even remember her name. I couldn't take it anymore. The pain inside of me was so deep it cut into my soul. I didn't feel like one person in the world saw me anymore. I felt worthless, unloved, unwanted, scared, confused about life, abandoned, hated. I had nothing but the clothes on my back. It was just me against the world now. I had no one in my corner. I had no kind of comforting feelings to tell me everything was going to be okay not any inspirations or happy thoughts. Why would God let these things happen to me repeatedly? Why has he abandoned me and let the darkness fill my soul? I wanted to die, I felt like there was no purpose in life for me anymore. My light was gone and I'm just alone in the dark now building up more and more darkness and confusion inside.

So by now I had been kicked out of both my parent's homes and other family member's homes because basically I was a rebel and no one understood me or took the time to try to figure out what was going on with me. I had nowhere to go. I would live with one of my friends till their parents found out I wasn't just staying a few nights and then I would move on to the next friend. I lived in one of my friend's closets, a garage, in a car & in other random places. I could just lay down my head down at night and fall asleep. Of course my granny let me stay with her a lot. She would feed me wash my clothes and pray for me and try to talk me to not doing whatever I was doing not really knowing what I was going through totally but at the same time she did. She still at that time never judged me or told me no, you can't come here. No way. Stay where you're at. You can't stay here. She never said those things. She just loved me unconditionally.

She knew my heart was claimed by the enemy and I was going through a hard season and wanted to help me. She did what she could whenever she could that being said I went to church with her. I promised I would go and I did a minimum of once a month. It didn't matter if I had stayed up all night the night before and I hadn't been to sleep. When I made a promise with my granny I tried to keep it. I loved that woman more than the air I breathed.

Now this church thing I had promised to do was hard for me to do but I did all the same. I was a little heathen but I went and I tried to listen to this preacher man stand in the pulpit and talk to us about God and life and good things and everything that God and Jesus wants for us but I heard none of it. I would sit right by her, but never hear anything and couldn't pay attention. My mind would wander off, my hands would swell up and I would start having an anxiety attack. I'd have pressure in my head and the room would start spinning as the weird looking things on the right of the bullpen would form and stare at me. The preacher would still continue to talk, because he had no clue what was manifesting by him and I would just sit there so freaked out I couldn't even move or speak. The devil was working against me; he didn't want me to hear what this man had to say because he knew it would change me.

I used to think it was that church my grandma went to but it was not the church that was making me have these issues, it was the devil trying to keep me from hearing or seeing what the preacher man was saying because they knew it would change my heart. So the enemy blocked my eyes and my ears from keeping that preacher man getting into my head. But I still continue to go with her. At least it I tried. I always didn't have a ride so I wouldn't have to walk or ride my bike or get dropped off if I wasn't at Grandma's house. I got there however I could possibly get there because I never wanted to hurt my granny or disappoint her.

Then finally I had a place to stay, I moved in with the three brothers temporarily. They were friends of mine I had known for a while. They let me stay there for free and fed me, I would go to school and party whatever I wanted and all I had to do was keep the house clean. That lasted for a few months until one night I came home from the beach all day then dinner with a friend. I was totally sober and tired. The boys were having a party so I just went into the room and passed out. A few hours later I woke up with one of them on top of me. They had a belt wrapped around me tight and a bible on my chest. The other brothers were in there and a room full of their guests whom I didn't know. They said I woke up my eyes looked weird and I started speaking in a weird language and freaking out.

I named everyone in the room there date of births and when they were going to die. I thought they were joking until they played the recording of me. So, it happened. That demon that had attached itself to me finally got in, but luckily the boys knew how to cast him out! Freaky very, very freaky and my chest hurt for months after that. I still don't know why. They didn't kick me out or anything. I just felt uncomfortable like it was time for me to leave. So that's what I did. I even thought it was not inside me anymore. It was not gone. I still felt it lingering around me waiting for its opportunity to get back in. It was a sly sneaky snake and preyed on me for many years after that.

Chapter 4

BOYS ARE TROUBLE

Eventually I got tired of running the streets so I asked if I could go on home please. Ninth grade was up on me now high school. This makes a new chapter in every child's life and is passed down from one generation to the next. The freshman experience hmmm... well I guess I just didn't see it all like that. I was seeing it as a prison for the next 4 long years and unhappy and unwilling time and chained in with all these other teenagers that were just like me, either smart, geeky, athletic, preppy, gangster, cowboy, or head bangers you would judge and place in one of these categories trying to fit in and find ourselves and I didn't really fit into one of the categories so I hung out with all of them.

Then you would float towards others like myself and interact with them. Everyone had their spot in school their trend to live by in the future to work towards. Me on the other hand I didn't really fall into any of the categories because I hung out with all of them. Each person did their thing in school and went to school every day. So, I'd get there and have an anxiety and a panic attack because I didn't really do well with the whole crowded hallways and chaos thing. There was always people yelling, fighting, flirting with people, and talking trash to people. Crazy hormonal teenager things just didn't work out with me very well. Yes, I know now that was a bad move. I should have just dealt with it like the rest the kids but I can't turn back the clock no matter how much I want to. I guess I was the opposite of normal still any way's, I was at 3 different high schools within a 2 year period, before I dropped out.

During this time I met my first real boyfriend Trent. I went home from school one day and was walking up the driveway and saw this truck sitting there. I was like okay we have company great. Then my brother pops out of the garage with his friend. The truck didn't belong to him. I continued walking up the driveway talking to them when this boy walks around the corner. I look at him and I couldn't breathe. I couldn't move. I stopped. The world around me stopped. I was floored by his presence. I stayed there for what seemed like an eternity. As they walk towards me, all I could do was to keep blinking, my mouth was wide open, and I was thinking I hope I look okay? In my mind I had no idea what was going on. My breath was gone. I was looking at his big green eyes, his long dark hair the way he pranced towards me. I was just in a state of awe ladies and gentlemen. Yes it's hard to believe I know, but at that moment I knew he was going to be my boyfriend.

So anyways I snapped out of it, closed my mouth and started to walk past him straight into my house and ignore that hot mess of a boy. Probably because I couldn't speak because, I became shy for the first time ever. I could not contain myself. I knew where they were headed, so I called over to my brothers other friend and asked for my brother and I said hey, who was that guy with you? But of course being the protector that my brother was he would not tell me anything because he knew this hotness of a guy was trouble. Plus he did not like me dating, especially any of his friends. We we're like any typical brother and sister we would have our fights but would always make up because we loved each other.

So I hung up the phone call back and ask for his friend that lived there. Unfortunately it was a land line because there were no cell phones back then, and yes folks, I'm old! Ha bubba in your face! Two can play that game. So his friend told me who mister green eye was and a few more details about him. Then I replied with ok so give him my number and tell him to call me when he gets home that I will be waiting. Some time went by that day but eventually he called me and we talked for hours. He was what my life became for years to come and I again had no clue what I was up against. Trent was my new best friend, partner in crime as you could say. He went with me and our friends on all of our little adventures the good and bad ones. We really had some good, bad times and just plain wild times, and I had finally found a piece of happiness in my dark world. He was not your typical guy of course. We would fight, break up, and then get back together. I would call him and stalk him until he would talk to me. We would take long drives and talk because my heart felt even more empty without him. My heart had been broken in half.

My life was not my own anymore it was his and I was not going to accept this as my reality. As any crazy teenage girl would do I stalked him and I never gave up and we had the same friends so I knew where he was going and what he was doing all the time. I only had eyes for him I found out quick he did not have the same eyes just for me and I didn't care. I planned to change his mind. I wanted to be with this boy forever. I wanted to marry him and spend my life with him. I went through good times and bad times and we would spend hours upon hours talking and driving around in his car listening to music and talking. It was like a cycle every time we broke up we did this.

Then when I turned 16 almost 17, I got pregnant. I was so happy. I knew this was fate. I had my baby boys name picked out. His name was going to be Jonathan Michael. I was ready to start my family with my man. Unfortunately my parents didn't think the same way. When they found out they told me I had to get an abortion or move out! I was crushed. I didn't know what to do or say. I had nowhere to go especially being pregnant and his parents would not let me move in because we weren't married and he really didn't want a baby either. This was so hard for me. My heart was torn in two. My heart was sunk deep into my chest as I rubbed on my belly thinking about my little bean inside of me. I couldn't breathe, my life was over I was sad and mad at everyone, and I was crushed. Why would they do this to me? It's not fair! No way was I giving up my baby. They are crazy! With or without him and my parents or his parents, I was going to keep this baby and raise it on the streets.

Then reality hit me. I was 16 I had no car no money no were to go because I had already stayed with every one of my friends. The last time I got kicked out I could barely make it on my own. I had no choice but have an abortion. Wow how can a person kill their child, how can a parent force their child to kill their baby in their stomach? Why because I'm 16 or because there were no morals in our family? I don't really know to this day and to this day I still regret it and think back how and why I did that and how if I hadn't it would be different. My life will never be complete. That baby will always be a piece of my heart a missing puzzle piece in my life. I cried for months upon months after that. I was traumatized. Jonathan Michael would be 20years old now if I hadn't aborted him. Wow 20 years old. Those kinds of decisions can't be taken back, it's something you have to live with and deal with for the rest of your life then one day have to face that baby again when you get to heaven.

Life is a precious gift and God gave me that baby as a gift to take care of and I just let him die because I wasn't strong enough to fight for hi, because I was weak minded, scared, and lost in the world around me so I murdered my child, which is a sin also. Just because it isn't born doesn't mean it isn't alive inside of you. Period, no matter what anyone says the baby has a soul to. Ladies don't ever let anyone make decisions for you, open up your mind and be strong; don't live with regrets for the rest of your life. If you don't think you can handle a baby then give it up for adoption to someone who is barren and can't have kids. There are plenty of other options beside abortion.

Anyways, I finally had to move forward in the darkness that surrounded me once again. I dropped out of school and got my G.E.D. I got a job and Trent and I got a little bitty apartment with all used hand me down stuff, but it was our own place. We lived there for a while partying every night doing the same thing as before. We lost that apartment and we moved into another but eventually the same thing happened. We lost it to. He moved back home and I moved into my own place. We still saw each other, but both were dating other people at that point. It was the same scenario as usual. Break up, get back together. It had become a broken record. We had some really good times and I made some life time friends that I will always love and cherish. But I just couldn't make it on the job I had, so a friend of mine I had met through friends and I started stripping on the weekends to make extra money. It was the hardest thing I've ever done. It was an all-time low for me. I didn't like my skinny body then and I don't like my big round booty now, so getting naked in front of random people sure wasn't my thing. I didn't even like getting naked in front of my boyfriend. I had to get drunker then a skunk or high before I could dance on stage naked! It was degrading, embarrassing and I was ashamed for doing it, but I had to survive, I had nowhere to go, no one to lean on, it was me against the world at this point in my life. I couldn't go home anymore nor did I want to. I couldn't understand how some of these girls could do this day in and day out like it was no problem, but who was I to judge I was doing it too. Life sure felt like I was living on the Jerry Springer TV show. I felt like I was gasping for air but barely being able to breathe. I was on a downward spiral sleeping all day and up all night, living in the dark shadows of the night, totally consumed by the world.

I totally hated stripping as you know, so I finally quit and got a job waitressing part time and working for an inventory company going into store and scanning everything in it. I lived next door to my best friend and around the pool down stair was a few of our other friends also it was like our own personal Melrose place. I was still partying and having fun filled crazy times with my friends, and I was still full of the darkness that surrounded me. But at least I had my own place and was trying to be responsible on some levels and becoming stable for the first time ever.

Chapter 5

MOVING FORWARD

Then it happened again, I was now 20 years old, I have lost my job, lost my apartment, and my car was broke down, so I had to move back home because I was pregnant with his baby again. But this time no one could tell me you can't have this baby! I decided I was keeping it and that's it! I had no clue what was in store for me or what I was going to do with no money, no job having to live with my parents again I was just a kid myself. I was confused. I was scared, I was alone because my boyfriend had done run off with another girl and I didn't know what I was going to do with my baby and me. The emotions hit me hard. What was supposed to be a happy time was a sad time because my baby hadn't even been born and our family had already been torn apart. I sobered up for the pregnancy of course. As soon as I found out I stopped everything. I was thinking clearly. But I was a train wreck I was a 20 year old drop out who was uneducated unstable unhappy dark young adult if I could even call myself that.

The only thing I had going for me was my parents let me stay with them and got me a new job at a theater. I would go to work and come home and lie in bed and cry for hours. Days and months went by just like that. I was broken totally broke the enemy had one. I was done. I didn't care about anything at all. I was back to going through the motions like a zombie every day. It was hard to even breathe I didn't want my daughter to grow up alone because I knew just how that felt and I had doomed her from the get go. Good mom I was starting out to be. I grew and grew and grew until I could not even see my feet. I tell you what young ladies it's not all what you think it is! Being pregnant hurts and it's not fun! Yes it's exciting and I loved being pregnant at first till my belly grew so big and the baby kicked like hard. She was a strong kid and I loved her. She was what I had to live for now. She gave me hope and dreams of what a better life was to come even if it would be just the two of us.

I continued to work and kept to myself with the exception of my few friends. I was torn still about my ex. I was grief stricken, lost, and hurt. I felt rejected and unloved not just for me but my baby. I prayed things would get better and change for my baby girl who I absolutely adored inside my belly. Then it was time. She was coming. I went to the dr. and he said she is not turning that they would have to turn her. Let me tell you about that. No way did I think they were going to turn my belly from the outside. Talk about excruciating pain. They tried turning her for what seemed like an hour but she wouldn't budge. Hmm go figure stubborn like her momma already. So they had to do a C-section. They finally got the baby out then the doctor is working and he yells to my mom; bring over your camera and take a picture of uterus its heart shaped! He was so excited because apparently it is very rare and why she wouldn't turn. All I could mumble was can you hurry up and finish and get me sewn back up? Wow all my glory is laid out everywhere and you people are standing around taking pictures.

Seriously just clean up my baby and show her to me. I'm mean really how would they like to be laying there all open? Finally he finishes and they bring her to me. She was perfect and beautiful and just perfect. Big bright blue eyes and a smile that was perfect she was just so stinking cute. I was in love with her from the moment I laid eyes on her. They took her and cleaned her up and said she was a perfect healthy little girl, and did I mention she looked like a little cabbage patch kid but alive and crying and moving around. I fell in love with her instantly. I knew my life would be different from this point forward. I would now have a purpose in life and that was my new little girl.

But I was losing blood and my blood pressure had dropped. You see that's why we don't stop to take pictures during a surgery of any sort just saying people. So they did an ultrasound and found that you get this, the doctor missed a stitch! Hmmm I wonder how that happened. Yep so I was bleeding internally in my incision which meant that it would eventually stop but I was losing a lot of blood so they had to give me more for one, for two weeks later that incision would pop and all that blood had to come out. This was supposed to be an experience of a lifetime, yeah right. Four days later, my baby and I went home and I am so grateful for my parents stepping up and being there for me because boy was I in pain after that bad surgery.

Oh ladies and gentlemen it gets worse the baby was very colicky she threw up everything it was like the exorcist was in her belly, plus no sleep for her or I, till finally many, many weeks later we figured out she was lactose intolerant. Yes 6 weeks of blissfulness. We survived it and both were finally healthy and happy. But I wouldn't have traded it for anything. She was my sweet perfect baby girl.

It was time for me to go back to work, I had become a manager at the theater and they needed me back over there. Life had finally started to look up. My baby and I were healthy had a roof over our heads and food in our bellies plus my parents had finally accepted me back in their lives. I was actually trying to do right in my life and be a responsible young adult. Working and taking care of my daughter was all I did for the next few months, just trying to push forwards with our lives and find our way through the world.

Chapter 6

CRAWLING BACKWARDS

Remember that piece that went missing during my pregnancy? Well it was back. It showed up one day out of the blue wanting to see the baby, & of course I let him. He had moved back home with his parents and left that girl and said he wanted to be with us... Well at first I was not about it at all because not only has he hurt me but he had abandoned and hurt my baby also but I loved him and I wanted things to work out for my little girl so we got back together but lived apart and tried to just work on things living separately. Things were going good. My baby girl was getting bigger and was the perfect child. I had a new office job Monday through Friday making good money. But I kept getting sick and I couldn't figure out why.

So I went to the doctor because something was wrong with my stomach. I told him I thought I had stomach flu. It was no stomach flu take a guess go on. Yes I was pregnant again. I was in shock but I was actually happy and excited for another bundle of joy to about to become a part of my little family. So I went home and told him before I sprung the news on our parents. We decided to get married and get our own place, because it was time. We got a little apartment then got married real quickly before our new little addition was born another girl.

Yes I was so excited and happy that life had worked it's self out. We started going to church with his parents both had jobs and trying to build our lives together. I was getting bigger every day. Then granny got sick. She was in and out of the hospital; they finally had to put her in a nursing home. So we tried to visit as much as possible. My mom would come over and pick up my daughter and I at least once a week and we would go see granny then me maw and pop.

So as usual mom came to get my daughter and me, and the new baby was almost here and I wanted to see my grandparents before I couldn't for a while. Plus I had a bad dream that woke me up the night before and I sweaty and in tears because I had dreamed granny was going to heaven. I had a bad feeling all morning about granny so Mom showed up to pick up my daughter and I, and she asked she me who you want to go see first me maw & pop or granny. I said well granny is gone and I don't want to go there and get thrown into labor by walking into that, so let's go see me maw & pop. Mom thought I was nuts and said we would have gotten a call if that was true but ok we will go to pops first. We got to me maw & pops and we're hanging out playing with the baby and the phone rang. My heart sunk into my stomach. I looked at my mom and said it's time. The room got so quite we could have heard a pin drop trying to listen in on the call. It seemed like forever until pop finally hung up the phone. I was praying for it to be anything but what I feared. Pop just looked over at us and said two words mom died. I fell to pieces right there. My heart was heavy. I had just lost the most amazing loving kind giving caring God fearing woman in my life. The only person I could totally trust and had faith in. Plus I was pregnant so my new baby girl wouldn't ever get to meet this amazing woman.

Although it hurt and I was deeply upset, I knew she had gone to heaven to be with the lord. Plus we were so close that we had talks about this situation and was prepared because every time I left I would hug her tight tell her I loved her and not to forget about me that she would have to come visit us and watch over the kids and I. Never the less I was prepared and had gotten to say my good bye but it didn't take the pain away. I still cry and miss her to this day. She was my hero, my rock, my everything.

Months, went by and I was starting to show more and more, I looked like a round watermelon, I would have to wobble around, couldn't see my feet and it was hard for me to move around even at all. I was as big as a house, and it was time for this baby to get out of my tummy! I was ready to meet my new little princess. This time the doctor scheduled another C-section and it went going quick. I was nervous of course because surgery is surgery, and I was nervous about meeting my new baby. So they prepared me and him for everything, we went into surgery and the anesthesiologist and the doctor did there thing quickly, and before I knew it I could hear my baby crying and laughing and smiles everywhere. The suspense was killing me. It took them forever to bring her over to me but finally they did. She was perfect oh she was a fat round baby with dark hair and blue eyes and perfect from her head to her toes, and totally didn't look like her sister so I was like is that my baby. I even asked them is this my baby? They laughed and said yes of course. She did not look like her sister at all, it was like night and day, but she was an amazingly beautiful sweet perfect little angel. I fell in love with her too from the moment I saw her. I just stared at her amazed at how cute she was, another cabbage patch kid! My life was now perfect. I had my two babies and my husband by my side. Everything seemed to be in place.

We brought her home and I would just stare at her and her sister for hours as they slept. I loved them so much and wanted them to have everything I didn't, I wanted them to have awesome childhoods and grow up to be leaders and have a great lives with no worries or problems. They were my pretty little princesses and my world my everything now and I loved my babies all the way to heaven and back.

They were growing fast. The baby was crawling and walking before we knew it so we had to move into a bigger place. So we got a rental house in his parent's neighborhood. He had a job working in the plants and I would watch the kids during the day and I started back in school and had a part time job at night. Everything was going good, we had our struggles but it seemed ok. Life seemed almost perfect. We never, not one time, argued or fought. I know that sounds strange but we just didn't talk about our problems at all like they weren't there.

The girls were happy and always having fun. My mom would come over and hang out with us during the day and play with the girls. We would go to the park, Mc Donald's, go shopping and swimming, and whatever we could do we did. The girls would go to his moms a lot also. His mom adored the girls. She absolutely loved them to pieces! They would stay nights and weekends with his mom and dad, which was okay with us because it was right down the street if they needed us. But then we started drinking and partying again when they were gone. We would have parties and started dabbling back into the drugs. I started feeling weird inside again, and that darkness was creeping back slowly. Our relationship started to change although we never talked about it, we both felt it.

He was taking more and more jobs out of town and leaving me home with the girls. So I just continued to do my thing, work school and kids. My brother had come to stay with us for a while so he kept me company. My brother kept telling my husband was cheating on me, but I didn't want to believe it. Then out of the blue my husband's dad died. He died in his sleep. It was horrible, unexpected and super sad and hard for all of us. We knew he went to heaven because he was a Godly man, but it didn't help the pain. He was a good man. He would always come over and visit the girls and me and wanted to see them all the time.

The girls didn't understand of course what had happened, and they kept telling me pawpaw was visiting them in their room. Then one day I was working in my room on homework and they girls were playing in their room, when it got quite. I heard my oldest daughter start talking. She was saying yes, I know, yes, I know, I love you to, I miss you to. I was like ok and started paying more attention to this one sided conversation. Then I heard this old raspy voice, that you can barley understand because when he was alive he had throat cancer and the surgery caused him to talk funny. It was one you could recognize easily and was very familiar, it was my husband's dad's voice. So I sprang up and yelled in there hey pawpaw come in here and talk to me to! Nothing happened and it got quite again, then the girls came running into my room and said mommy you made pawpaw leave. That wasn't the last experience they had like that, either. So I was like wow, I jumped up and ran into the living room where my husband was playing video games and told him. He was like whatever. He was not handling his death well at all and he was not showing any kind of emotions as usual, so I don't know what was going on in his mind. But our relationship after that hit a landslide.

After a few weeks went by he took another job out of town as usual. Then one Friday he came home out of the blue, said hi to everyone, took a shower, got dressed, grabbed some of our condoms and left. He said he had plans and had to work that next morning. I was dumb founded. My heart was broken into pieces and had sunk into my stomach, this couldn't be happening again. We talked about this before we got married, and he promised he wouldn't do this. I just didn't know what to say or think. I stewed over it and decided I wasn't going to give up. So I confronted him, and he denied it of course, he wouldn't talk to me about anything. So I tried talking to him more, tried to get him to go to counseling with me. I wanted nothing more than my family to be happy and stay together. I did not want my kids to have to endure a divorce like my brother and I had to. Fear had set in me deeply, I was terrified of what was to come, and I felt really horrible for my girls. They were so little that they really wouldn't even know what was going on, but still. They would be ripped away from that happy little lifestyle we had.

We struggled for the next few months trying to salvage what we had, but nothing seemed to work. He quit working and we couldn't afford our home anymore, so he wanted to move back home with his mom, well he did and I ended up getting a little two bedroom apartment with my brother and the girls that my dad helped us get. It happened, the worst fear I have had in years. We ended up separating, then getting a divorce. I kept the girls still worked and was still going to school. But the darkness was clouding up above my head again; I was hurting again all that pain I used to have came flooding back. There was a huge hole in my heart, not only for me but for my daughters. I felt so horrible, I felt like a failure as a mom and a wife. I was worthless, unwanted and unloved again. I didn't know what to do with myself so I just continued what I was doing. I would do my best to hold it together in front of the girls and everyone, but I would lie in bed at night and cry myself to sleep full of hate, fear, sadness and remorse. I had no clue what I was going to do and no idea what our futures had to hold. What of their little lives now and there futures? I was traumatized. My heart was broken into thousands of tiny pieces. My life was over as far as I was concerned. I was now just living for my baby girls.

Chapter 7

THE PERFECT STORM

Trying to adjust to our new way of life came way easier for the girls. They took everything in stride and as an adventure. I really don't think they understood what happened to be honest, because they were so little. I on the other hand did not. I was depressed, scared, miserable, and unsure of what was going to happen to us. I felt unloved, unwanted, rejected, and I felt like a failure as a wife and mother. It's like a hurricane whipped through our lives without asking and destroyed everything possible in its path. Touching down right where it knew it would hurt the most, not caring if we survived or not. Tearing everything apart all at once, making everything fall apart with no way to fix it, leaving me standing in the midst of a storm, falling apart, with two children on my hips.

A dark cloud was over my head. I felt nothing, besides pain and misery inside. I knew I would never be with my husband again. Wow, I will never be with my husband again. It sank in deep now. I knew our family was over, and I knew my kids were doomed. I grew up in a divorced home and I barely survived it. I never ever wanted this for my kids. I didn't want them to have to ever walk the path I walked. Not even a little of it. It takes a mom and a dad to raise children they need both their parents there for them no matter what. How was I going to do this on my own? I had no clue at all. I could barely manage with my husband helping me. What do I say or do now? Just live day to day and watch my kids grow up before my eyes while I'm stuck in a twilight zone. Not sure of myself, feeling confused and lost with no idea what to do. I couldn't wrap it around in my brain at all, it was like a jig saw puzzle with missing pieces.

Of course I kept everything inside and never let the kids see what was wrong with me. Now I am in a small two bedroom apartment with my two daughters and my brother. I still woke up every day and went to work and school. My brother kept the kids for me while I went to school and work, unless they were at their dads. I started a downward spiral again. If they were gone or asleep after I got home from work, I would go out with my friends or whoever I could find to chill with. This started to become a regular thing. I started slipping back into my old habits again and not thinking about what was good or bad. It's not what I should be doing at all with myself. I was doing all the wrong things instead of the right things. Drinking, staying out late, dabbling back into drugs, hanging out with the wrong crowd. I had no one there telling me anything different or that what I was doing was not okay. I had no support system, no one to tell me to snap out of it and push through the pain, or that everything would be alright. I had no one telling me that this is just a season for the girls and me. No I was alone again. People were all around me all the time but I felt alone. Yes my brother was living with me, I had friends, and family, but I couldn't confide in anyone.

I had still not told anyone what all I had been through and it was all flooding back in me again like the oceans waves creeping up to the shore hitting me in the face and into my soul. All my old demons were back and torturing me. My thoughts were becoming insane. It's like I could not breathe anymore. My chest was hurting the whole was back. I was freaking out inside and torturing myself. I was becoming numb inside again and I was just going through the motions every day. I had begun to have the just fake it till I make it kind of feelings towards life. I was drowning in my own pool of sins that had built up more and more over the years and I was scared it would rub off on my daughters.

Every day that passed I would wake up, open my eyes and stare at my daughters in amazement. They were perfect, precious, beautiful princesses, and I loved them with every inch of my soul. Words cannot express the love I have for my kids. They were my rock, my everything, and my reason to keep going, my reason for living. Their perfect little laughs and smiles were soothing to me. It made me realize that there is hope of some sort still out there somewhere. I was ashamed of myself and I did not like the person I was becoming again. I was miserable in my own web that I had spun myself. My choice selection was slim to none, because I wasn't thinking rationally what so ever. I seemed legit on paper and to the people around me. I had a tough girl attitude, working and going to school. Yes, that was all smoke screens and mirrors though. I didn't walk a straight line it was curved; it zigged and zagged, went in circles and had no end in sight. My head was clouded and my judgment was gone on a field trip to Disney land with peter pan to never land. But, I was still alive and felt my heart beating harder and harder every day, like it was trying to tell me everything was going to be ok, or maybe it was the drugs. Either way, I wasn't going to fail my kids, so I still tried a little every day to smile and show them I loved them. Even in the midst of all my chaos in my head and life, I loved my kids and wanted what was the best for them always, so I would continue my life for them, and live everyday with this misery and pain inside of me was growing stronger and stronger, feeling abandoned and lost, the pain rose from my stomach into my throat suffocating me till I couldn't breathe, the demon's were perching on my shoulders again waiting for me to turn back to them again. I was slowly slipping away and becoming just a shadow girl living in the dark world again.

Chapter 8

LOVE STRIKES AGAIN

I've been working at the bowling alley for a while now. I worked every night and every weekend. I worked the leagues and open bowl every night and helped close the place down. I knew almost everyone that came through the doors in that place except, him. One night during Friday night league he walked up to me, he looked me dead in my eyes and said these seven little words. I'm going to marry you one day. I couldn't speak so I just rolled my eyes and played it cool then looked the other way. I thought to myself, say what home fry? What, what? Wow I was just, I couldn't speak. He was so cute and good looking and he wanted to marry me. What no way. What a good pick up line I thought, and well it worked. I was dumb founded by this boy that just literally walked up and into my life. He had brown hair, brown eyes, and a goatee with the Charlie sheen looking bowling shirt and khaki pants in all. That's it I knew from that moment also that I was going to be with this boy. He was single with no kids but he loved kids so that was a good thing since I had two girls. He had a job and lived with his parents.

We did the whole flirt back and forth thing and exchanged numbers. We started to text and talked on the phone constantly for hours at a time from morning till night. I was starting to smile again a little. I felt like things could actually be getting better. Things moved very fast though. He took me on my first real date and treated me like a lady should be treated, opened doors for me, brought me flowers to work, pampered me, ran the bath water for me, even painted my toe nails for me. He was something I had never experienced and I fell in love with him fast. I honestly thought I was going to be single forever and didn't expect this.

I introduced him to the kids and they loved him. They got along great. He started spending nights with us, and spending time with the girls. Then he moved in with us within months. We were a family. It was a new start together and with my daughters. He was such a good man and treated the girls like they were his own. I was just amazed and in love with everything about him.

We spent all of our time together and with the girls. I continued to work and go to school. Things were going good. We had a happy little family. Summer came we went on camping trips and enjoyed life as it was, it was the little things. The girls were starting to get big my oldest was starting pre K, school. I couldn't believe how time was flying. We had almost been together a year. Everything seemed perfect. Before I knew it thanksgiving and Christmas was here so we spent our first official holidays together with our families, the kids were happy and so was I. New Year's came again we spent it with the girls.

Now it's January, which a lot goes on this time of year, we have oldest daughters, my dad, uncles, nephews and others all birthdays. First of the year stuff to do, clean up and go through the old and make room for all the new stuff, it's just a busy month. So busy I didn't realize that I missed my period. That's right America I missed my period. I was emotional, hormonal, and being a grouchy pants like nobody's business. I couldn't figure out what was going on with me. Then, I realized I hadn't had my period since before Christmas, so I bought a pregnancy test. BAM I was pregnant!

My boyfriend was totally excited! This was his first and only child. He would rub my belly and talk to it, sing and read to it. It was very sweet and cute. He smiled nonstop. So did I, our little family was going to be perfect and it was a boy! So the girls would have a sweet little brother. I was completely happy. Moody and grouchy, but happy. It had to be the boy hormones running through me because when I was pregnant with the girls I was happy throughout my pregnancy but not with my son. I felt like slapping everyone every day. I couldn't get full, I stayed hungry, grouchy, and just mad. It was totally weird. We ended up moving out of that little apartment and into his parents' house to save money. We stayed there until right before the baby was born. Then we got an apartment in another city 30 minutes from my family and friends. I did not like it out there not one bit.

Everything went horrible out there. The apartments had issues with their water system and lights, the kids couldn't go outside because it was a bad area, the school bus kept forgetting my youngest daughter at school and I would freak out and have to go find her. We didn't have cell phones or home phones so I had to go to a pay phone to call anyone. I was nesting, so I would be constantly on my feet cleaning and rearranging everything, on top of being a big fat, hormonal, emotional, pregnant woman. I couldn't see my feet I was so big, I had to roll off the couch and the bed onto the floor to get up, I was a big rolly, polly with the on the edge CRAZY LADY ISSUES just ready to pop out that baby as soon as possible!

Finally September rolled around, and it was time to have my baby. Same doctor that delivered the girls was about to deliver my son on scheduled C-section. We were totally excited and I knew everything was going to go good. Well I hoped. Everyone was up there waiting for him to come. We go in and everything was going smooth so far. Then the anesthesiologist comes in and gets ready to numb me and misses his mark, the pain was excruciating, I was getting upset now, then he does it again and was like hold still ma'am. Dude I am not moving its alllll you! Ugh… I was upset now and told him if he missed this time I'm coming off this table swinging! So the third time he finally gets the needle in my back correctly and I felt the medicine running down into my spine. I began to hyper ventilating a lot and I could feel the doctor cutting me open, the medicine wasn't working so they had to numb me more. That was so scary! So they bring in my boyfriend in and they get ready to pull out my son I'm I just lying there trying not to be sick after that LITTLE INCIDENT with a air mask on now and he is just about bouncing off the walls with excitement.

Then the doctor said hey man, come over here and cut the cord. So he did and then I heard the baby cry. I cried tears of joy and my heart was filled with warmth. A few minutes later my man brings the baby over to me so I can see him. The baby and I locked eyes, and I fell straight in love with him like I did with the girls. He was perfect, healthy, adorable, and a handsome little boy. He had Brown hair, blue eyes, and chubby cute cheeks, another cabbage patch kid. Our family was complete so I told the doctor. Tie me up doc this garage is now closed! So they tied my tubes because I finally had all the babies I needed. My three little loves who have my heart forever and we're all here and I loved them more then the air I breathed I loved them all the way to heaven and back.

My man took the baby out into the hallway to show our family. They were all excited and taking pictures. My dad walked up and said he is so stinking cute and looks just like ex-husband, Jeremy's mouth dropped open and he almost dropped the baby till my dad said nah man I'm just kidding he looks like you. Oh my goodness my dad the jokester! So finally I got to hold him after waiting which seemed like forever, and he was just so perfect and cute. He was going to be a heart breaking handsome young man. His sisters got to meet him and hold him. They made up songs to sing to him and constantly was hugging and kissing him. We were a perfect little family.

I finally got to go home after a few days, and boy was I ready. My dad picked us up and we detoured to his house for little while to visit before he took us all the way home because I wouldn't be going anywhere anytime soon. Then we got home, and I got to put him in his little bed and lay down without having to roll off to get up! Yes! I was back to my normal non hormonal crazy self. Thank goodness that was over and my little man was just perfect. One cannot express the love you have for your children. There're no words you can say or nothing you can do to express your love for your child, all I know is that my heart belongs to them and will always belong to them no matter how big they get. My three little loves were all perfect and I loved them all the way to heaven and back. My family was now complete, and we were happy and complete finally for the first time since I was a child. Life was looking up and becoming the perfect life I had always dreamed of.

Chapter 9

WHERE DO WE GO NOW?

The next few months were up and down for me. I was happy and sad, the doctor had put me on an anti-depressant medication for postpartum depression to help me feel better but I didn't like the reaction it gave me so I quit taking them. I figured it was because I had my hands full with three kids now, and no one to help me or support what I was going through. I felt alone. I know my son's dad was there and he did help with things but I felt alone and isolated from the world.

I wasn't working because I was on my six weeks stay at home time with the baby. On a daily basis it was just the kids and I. No one to talk to no one to vent to, and I couldn't even go use the pay phone because the baby was too little to be taking outside still. I was happy to have alone time with my little family because I loved them all so very much. But I was craving adult conversations. And I was missing my family and my friends. Living in a different town from everyone is one thing but not being able to communicate to anyone at all, for instance just call and talk to them not even my parents. I felt like I was totally alone, unloved unwanted and disconnected from the world and the ones I loved. It's important to me to be around family especially when you have little kids. They need their family all of them not just their mom, dad, brother and sisters.

People are not built to be alone, they're built to have other people around them, talk, vent, tell stories, and have bonding time, eat dinner together, and just do things together, especially since I'm a social butterfly. I love being around the ones I love and my close friends. Some people chose to isolate themselves but I'm not that kind of person. I need to have interactions with others at least sometimes. I know we all get busy in our lives and forget about others and don't have time to socialize but to me those things are precious. I would go crazy without it.

This time went by slow but before I knew it the six weeks were over and I was able to go back to work. Unfortunately the place I was working did not hold my position, so now I had to seek out a new job. Jeremy was running his own side business and it was not busy so we had to end up moving into his parents' house until we could figure out what to do. Yep, Jeremy and I plus our now 3 kids had to do what we had to do in able to survive as a family. We crammed into their little trailer with the two of them and their other granddaughter who lived with them. So his parents in one room, their granddaughter and my girls all shared a room, and then my man, the baby and I in another. The rooms were super tiny and it was hard but we all made it through it. The next few months were very hard for me. I didn't get back to work till after the first of the year. I'm not one that likes to sit at home at all. I like to work and stay busy. So since my job was gone my mom got me on with the company she worked for in the plants as a fire watch. The job I was working was an hour away, and the jeep we had was falling apart I had to pray my way to work and home every day.

Finally I saved up to put down on a Van and we started looking for our own place. I was jumping from one job to the next trying to stay busy and save money to get our little family ahead, while he stayed home with the kids. I did this for a few years we ended up getting a nice trailer of our own and everything was starting to finally come together. I started working even more now and out of town all over the country I started traveling. My son and Jeremy would normally go with me out of town and my daughters would stay with their grandma. I moved up from fire watch to helper then tool room attendant within months. I loved this kind of work and the money wasn't shabby either.

Then it happened, the craziness started. There was a black cloud floating over our home. We started to fight constantly, yelling and screaming even with my kids at home. He believed that I was cheating on him out in the plants when in reality I was just trying to make money and put food on the table and clothes on our backs. Anytime

I went to work he got suspicious and started a huge fight. He didn't want me to go out of town on my own, but he couldn't go because the girls were in school now. He would call me names and cut me down till I felt as big as an ant. Then I finally had enough I drew a line one night when we were in the kitchen and he cornered me up against the cabinets and told me if I LEAVE HE WOULD CUT MY HEAD OFF AND POOP DOWN MY THROAT! I was freaking out inside, and cornered up against the kitchen cabinet. So in defense I hit him as hard as I could in the face, well he hit me back just as hard and gave me a black eye. I was in tears crying I hit the floor and he was still screaming at me. I couldn't think or breath I was scared for my life. Finally he stopped and I got up and went to bed. The next day I left for my job and was gone for three weeks. That was fun trying to explain how I gave myself a black eye to my coworkers. That was the only time he hit me, but the mental games had just begun.

He was always a pot head but started doing coke with his golf buddy; eventually I did it to along with him because at that point I felt like I was trapped. I couldn't breathe or even think for myself anymore, any move I made I got reprimanded like a child. I couldn't or wouldn't leave for one because I wanted my kids to have a chance at actually having a family and for two because he had made me feel like no one else would ever love me, or want me, that I was the scum on the bottom of his shoe, constantly in my face yelling and screaming at me and threatening me if I ever left him and took his son I would pay for it. I had gained tons of weight and he made sure to remind me of it daily, he would force me to have sex with him, and nights we would drink and carry on and I would pass out or black out, then I would wake up naked the next morning sore from him having his way with me and find random house things shoved in me that he would use for his pleasure on me. Not to mention the mental abuse was so bad I couldn't even think straight, I didn't know pain was till I could barely look at myself in the mirror with tears streaming down my face, mad, hurt, and begging myself to hold on another day, to be strong, and think about my babies.

Anyways I quit working out in the plants because of all the madness and went back to work for my dad. We had lost our trailer so I moved in with my dad and he moved in again with his parents, because I wasn't sure what I needed or wanted. After a few months I got an apartment with the kids. He and I were still seeing each other of course but I needed time to think. I lost it I was going crazy, I can own that now, I was crushed because everything was happening again like before with my ex husband. I loved him so much I couldn't stand the pain; it hurt so deep it felt like someone was cutting me with a jagged edged knife in little slits slowly. I couldn't take it.

My life had been flipped upside down and I had no clue what to do or how to live anymore. My heartfelt broken and empty like it was just a shell with nothing in it. The pain was so severe that I had to mask it with alcohol and drugs, we broke up and I started messing around with other men, not even caring about anything or the consequences that would fallow. A few months go by and we decided to try it again. I finally let him move back in because I felt lost, scared, and alone, there was a big hole in my heart and a felt like a void in my life and nothing and no one could make me happy so why not try again with Jeremy. I started working off and on in the plants still but he went with me everywhere. I went till eventually I got tired of it and just stayed working with my dad. We moved from that apartment into bigger apartment with the kids and his mom now, because her and her husband split up and she moved in with us because she was very sick with brain tumors. She had two twelve hour surgeries within that year, during which she had a stroke and almost died. So the stress levels were very high and I was scared not just for Jeremy but for my young son who hadn't gotten to really know his grandmother yet. She made it through and was recuperating with us helping her as much as we could. Everything seemed to be going ok besides that. I was back in school and working for dad. We both were trying to make things work for the kids I think.

Trying to keep things as normal as possible but we were still partying also. Don't get me wrong I did love him with all my heart even with all the issues we had been through but it was like a roller coaster ride. Things would be good then down we would go then back up then down again never knowing what was going to happen next. We both loved our kids very much. He treated the girls like his own and loved us all so much. But we couldn't move past all the damage that had happened. Sometimes words hurt so deep that it is imprinted inside your mind and soul and when you see or think about that person who hurt you it just brings back all those hurtful words.

Chapter 10

BLIND FOLDED

I felt on a daily basis like a walking zombie, get up get the kids all to school, go to work, come home cook dinner, go to school, lay with the kids put them to bed everyday day in and day out. I was oppressed, depressed, and didn't want to live any longer. I felt so numb and dead inside that nothing really mattered. I started to see a psychologist and it helped but it only lasted for a short time because after they saw me they wanted to do couples therapy and we just couldn't afford it. The last day I had went I was just pulling up about to go in when I get a call from his mom telling me he was in jail. The cops were going door to door looking for a runaway, well he answered the door not thinking and had a joint behind his ear. So they took him to jail. He got out that day but the apartments didn't like it.

Next it was my turn. We used to go out to the bars quite often. Just to get out of the house. We didn't ever worry about anything or repercussions not even thinking about the stuff that could happen. We went out for my buddy's home coming party, and had a fun night but on the way home we got into a huge argument. I was really light headed. Besides that some couple at the bar who was trying to take me home slipped me a Mickey so I started feeling weird about then. So we get home he runs inside and I get in the driver seat like I'm going to leave and instead of putting it in reveres I put it in drive gunned it because I was going to be cool and speed out of there and hit the gate to our patio. Yay... so I went inside saw everyone was ok and went back to the car to sit and think alone because now I know I'm not driving anywhere. So I decided to get the CD out of the radio and go in. Well just as I'm doing that a cop walks up on me. And takes me to jail for DWI because the keys were in the ignition and I could have the intent to drive. Wrong this white girl wasn't going anywhere!

So because of both those incidents the apartments kicked us out. So we moved into a house around the corner thanks to my good ole dad helping us out once again. So we all really liked the house it was even bigger and better then the apartment probably the best place we had lived yet. The kids were all in the school they liked, and had finally room to run around and play, and we made friends with the neighbors. It seemed like things were finally getting better. We were still doing all the same things as before but it seemed as if the air was starting to lift.

My best friend and I even decided to start going to church. We went to a few different ones trying to find the right fit but never did. I felt like I needed Jesus back in my life. We lived in that house just about a year. Boy then the trenches got deeper. I felt like I couldn't make a move we all walked on eggshells around him. He was now treating my daughters like he did to me, with the mental abuse and everything we did was horrible no matter what it was, he had me and the kids under his thumb boot camp style, but worse it never ended. His motto was to break us down to where we felt like we were nothing, then he was going to build us back up the way he thought we should be. Wrong! You're talking to a house full of Italian hard heads women here. He tore us all down but never built us back up. I would lay in the bathtub at night and think of ways I could kill myself just so I would be rid of this craziness. But every time I would think those horrible thoughts I would circle back around to the kids and leaving them to deal with life alone. So I never did it. My kids were my life. I may have not been being the best mommy in the world at this point, but I would have died for my kids.

People just don't understand when you're in a relationship with that kind of mentality you're not able to think of the future, of your kids, or how to get out of the situation you're in. Your brain has been rearranged to believe only what that person says. When you have been stripped down to nothing in your brain, when you are in such a state of depression and on drugs to top all that off, you are not thinking with a sound mind, not at all. But something inside me kept telling me I had to move forward that there is life outside of this chaos, and to be strong.

So the night it all ended, we were at the bowling alley for summer league, we had drank a bottle of alcohol and beers on top of that. On the way home again we started arguing, not just him and I but his mom was involved in it too taking up for her son of course which was the normal thing now. Well I had enough of being threatened and ganged up on. He threatened me for the last time. I called the cops then called my daddy to come get me and my kids. The cops had to be there or he wouldn't have let me leave and only God know what would have happened if I would have stayed. So I left then next day I informed him that I was getting my own house on my own over in my ex-husbands neighborhood and I was taking the kids all with me.

Chapter 11

THE FUTURE IS CALLING

Living week to week and check to check off one income was a hard thing to do. Not knowing if you can afford the things your children want or need and having to say no to everything they ask for makes you as a parent feel like you're not doing your job. I bit off more than I could chew getting a house on my own, but I didn't want to go backwards either. I made enough, but just enough to pay for the bills and things we needed and my dad would help me when he could also. It was not only hard being a single mom of three kids for the first time but it was lonely to. I didn't know how to feel or act, it was all new to me and scary.

I had been with the kid's two dads for the last 20 years. 10 years each. I was confused still from everything he had said and done and so were the girls. But how could I comfort them and make them feel better and safe when I couldn't even for myself. We were all on our last leg just trying to learn how to get back up and walk again. Our lives were torn apart shred by shred, our hearts had been broken and the pain was all we felt even my son. He just lost his mommy and daddy being together forever. He really couldn't understand because he was so small. All he saw was that we lived apart now. No more good night hugs and tickles and snuggled between us it was ripped away from him for my own selfish needs. I never wanted this to happen I wanted our family to stay together and work through it all. But there was no working through it, so I had to make the right decision for not only myself but for the kids to. I would lie in bed and cry at night till I fell asleep. My heart felt like it was just gone. Not even broken anymore but just ripped out of my chest and thrown in the trash.

So I continued to drink and do drugs to numb everything even more so than when I was awake. The light in my head was off like I was awake but wasn't really there. I felt so bad about everything I put my kids through that it haunted me in my thoughts and in my dreams, it was consuming me. I could not fix what I had done nor did I know how to change everything and make things right. I love my children more than the air I breathe more than the amount of time my heart can beat more than my life itself and I have failed them, miserably. I did it to my daughters and now I have done it to my son. I took my son out of his little happy home into a dark zone filled with ugly unforgiving darkness that had been draped over our home like a blanket as you sleep. It was so heavy and dark that I couldn't even begin to understand the depths of depression I was in.

So I would go to work come home cook clean hang out with the kids and then when they were all gone to their dads, I would go out with my friends, drink and do drugs till early in the morning and this went on for months. Then one night it happened, I dropped off my kids at their dads to spend time with him on my daughter's birthday and I went out. But I didn't stay out long because a friend of mine was coming home with me to get high, so I only had a few drinks, then about midnight we left the bar and headed to my house. I was driving my Toyota and he was on his chopper behind me. It was a road I had drove on a hundred times, nothing new. I looked down to turn the radio station and looked back up and bam I hit a truck that had slammed on its breaks for no reason and apparently its break lights didn't work. There was nothing in the road, no streets to turn on, nothing just fields. I hit the air bag then I hit the steering wheel three times after that. I blacked out for a few minutes and when I came to I was across the road and had no front end. I looked around and there was no one, not the truck I hit not the buddy that was fallowing me nothing. I couldn't move my leg hurt, my chest hurt, I was scared and didn't know what to do. I called my friends at the bar down the road to come get me, but by the time they got there the ambulance and cops had showed up. So I went to the hospital and stayed there for observation.

The next morning I was black and blue from my neck to my ankles, my right ankle was hurt and I was sore but I was okay. My buddy who was fallowing me had hit my bumper and flown off his bike and when he got up, he said he checked on me I was alive just knocked out, so he called the cops and left because he had warrant's. This wasn't my first wreck but it was my first big wreck the ones before this was just fender benders. This one was bad so bad the car was totaled. I was lucky to be alive the cops said because I had hit the steering wheel so many times that usually the person would of came up out of there seat belt and went through the window but I didn't. I was laid up for weeks, recovering, and waiting to get another vehicle but finally I did, I got a mountaineer and it was nice! Things seemed to be getting better, I was seeing a nice guy who I had really started to like, I was still in school and having to drive to Katy an hour away twice a week for my classes and back at work, the kids seemed to be doing better, everything seemed to be actually looking up.

Then it happened, I was driving to school one day on the beltway 8 almost to the toll booth to pay, and a BMW on his cell phone realized he was in the change lane not the EZ tag lane and pressed on the gas jumped over in front of me and clipped my front end sending me into the middle of the change and EZ tag lanes then flipping me over three time back against the wall. Thank goodness I had my seat belt on! My truck was totaled, most of the windows had been blown out, the whole outer body was shot again and I was hanging upside down still attached with my seat belt. I had hurt my ankle and I had glass stuck in me everywhere but I was ok. This time everything went in slow motion I saw everything happening around me, all the cars slowing down and the faces they were making, glass flying everywhere, my things flying everywhere, I could see and hear the noises and the truck crunching as it rolled, and then I saw my life flash before my eyes.

It all happened so fast, but it felt like forever. I could move at first I just hung there upside down and in shock, like it wasn't registering that I had been in another wreck. Then I heard voices saying ma'am are you okay? So I answered yes and did my best move I could as a spider monkey to unbuckle and flip myself back over and up out of the truck. The police and ambulance was on their way so I called the guy I was dating to come get me because I knew he was in the area, plumbers work everywhere! Wow I was blown away it had only been a month since my last wreck, and now I'm dealing with this again, but at least I was alive and unharmed besides bruises and being sore.

So it was back to square one on the vehicle situation, the guy I was seeing and I were starting to have problems because of his personal life, and I was running out of the money I had because I was spending it as fast as I got it on bills, cars, kids and my tattoos and my extracurricular activities. I was in love with him. He treated me better than any man had ever treated me. He was sweet, passionate, caring, opened doors for me, cooked for me and didn't yell or scream at me when I screwed up. He was very handsome and loved my kids. He was perfect so perfect I had gotten a tattoo with his bite marks on my shoulder to represent the love I had for him. But that wasn't enough for him, he had so much going on in his life that honestly, really I didn't fit in with it, so he found a girl that did and broke up with me. Well back downhill I went, I couldn't think I couldn't sleep or eat or get out of bed even. I just stayed in bed for weeks and cried. I thought he was the one and the rejection was so painful I couldn't bare it. I neglected my kids, my job, my house, everything

I finally got out of bed and kicked myself in the butt for that. I am a strong independent woman I don't cry over boys and never will again. So that ended that tragedy. We still remained friends and even tried to date again a few more times but it never worked out, which was for the best. After going under like that and having wrecks and not being able to work my bills started piling up, and I couldn't afford the house any longer. So the kids and I packed our things put it all in storage except our clothes and moved into my dad's beach house for the summer, because really we had no were else to go and I was not making enough money to rent a place.

Over the summer my cousin found out what had happened and offered for the kids and me to come stay with her and I could pay her a small amount a month so I could save money. This was a huge blessing. I felt so relieved and thankful that she actually understood what I was going through and was compassionate enough to let us stay in her home. So we moved in with her, right before school started again. I was still working for my dad and going to school, but I felt lost, incomplete and empty inside. I was back to going through the motions. I would take the kids to school; go to work, and school, every day like before. I didn't know what my future would hold. I was broken. Broken to the point I didn't care if I lived or died anymore. My heart, my mind, and my soul were damaged beyond repair. I was numb to everything and everyone. It was as if I was an empty shell, walking and talking but there was nothing happening inside. I slowly slipped back into drinking again, I began to go out a lot, partying with my friends, sleeping around with men, and doing drugs every chance I got. I was on a non-stop train to never land, and there were no refunds no exchanges and no way back. I was killing myself slowly. I had thoughts of suicide many times, just driving myself off the beltway 8 bridge or parking on the rail road tracks and passing out after a drunken night.

I felt like my kids and family would be better off without me. Who needed a loser like me in their life who was on a downward spiral so fast that was never going to get back up. I did more damage to myself and others then I did good. I felt worthless, Jeremy was right about all those things he used to say about me. I was a no good horrible bad person/mom, that was fat, lazy, inconsiderate, unworthy, and I didn't care about anything anymore. Boom that's when I thought I hit my all-time low! I was just a girl living in the shadows.

Chapter 12

THE WAKEUP CALL
FROM BEYOND

Months go by and I'm no different. The kids were all gone for the weekend to their dad's houses, so I decided to spend the weekend high. So I called up my dealer and told him to meet me at the usual location, the gas station near my house. I got there before him and as usual he was running late. So I just sat there sober, anxious, depressed and just starring out the window waiting. Then all of a sudden I heard a voice come through my speakers. It was a loud, deep, and stern voice that got my attention and scared me all at once. This man said: Daughter, I have watched you suffer long enough. It has broken my heart to see you living your life this way. So that's enough! I set a path for you long ago that you abandoned and I have a plan for you, and I need you now. You will never again touch drugs, you will do as I say, or you will pay the ultimate price.

I fell into a deep sleep and when I opened my eyes I was in the pits of hell. It was dark and hotter than a summer day in the dessert, there was no water to quench my thirst, and it felt like I was burning from inside out. There were loud agonizing screams coming from every direction, growls, roars, strange noises I have never even heard. I could hear fire burning all around me, and the smell was so retched I could hardly stand it. I was terrified beyond belief. I was standing in a line of people, against a cave like wall, one at a time they would step forward in front of this demon, that was probably 20 foot tall and built with long fingers and long sharp nails, its feet were big also with long sharp nails, it had horns its face was indescribable rough bumpy looking almost but its eyes were red. It would dip down and tear the person apart limb by limb with its horns and hands, piece by piece as they had to endure the pain, hitting them beating on them, raping them, whatever the demon felt like doing, as it laughed, and after he was done the person's body would pop up and back together, then they would go get back in the line again for the next round.

There was nowhere to run nowhere to hide, because they would find you and torture you worse. As the line moved forward I looked to my side and Jesus was standing by me. I said please, please, take me out of here, I don't want this, I'm scared Jesus, please I beg you. He didn't respond he just stood there watching me. I'm now having anxiety and panicking because I realized I was next. I could not move I just froze and stood there when the demon summoned me over. I couldn't do it, so he somehow pulled me over with a snap of his finger. He looked down at me with his big red eyes and smiled, like oh yeah fresh meat. I yelled Jesus if you take me out of here I will pledge my life to you and do whatever you say.

So he responded just as the demon started to dip down, and said okay. All of a sudden I was away from the demon, standing by Jesus again. He told me this, this is not a dream, this will be your reality very soon if you don't change your life. I have a plan for you, and if you do not stay on my path I have set for you then this will be your destiny. Now go home, and prepare yourself for what is in store.

I woke up, back in my van drenched in sweat, and it was now dark outside, hours had passed and the store had closed. No one even noticed I was asleep in my van. No one woke me up, or bothered me. It was like they couldn't see me there. I just sat there for a while thinking about what just happened. I couldn't wrap my brain around it. I had no clue what had just happened. I was in shock scared and afraid of what I had just witnessed. There were no words to describe how I was feeling, none, and nothing at all. So I turned on my van and went home. My dealer never showed up, and if he did, he either didn't see me or didn't wake me up. I went home, got in bed and just laid there for hours, never speaking of what happened to me, and never touching drugs again.

Months go by, and I just continue listening to what God told me, by staying sober and trying to be a better person. I didn't feel whole inside yet though. I still felt broken and unhappy but at least now my mind body and soul wasn't filled with extra junk that was being clouded up with drugs and alcohol. I was still living day to day not knowing what would be next. I started seeing my ex-boyfriend Jeremy again my son's dad, spending time with him and my son and staying over there a lot. I wanted to give him one more shot, since I was now sober. I figured I could help him get sober also. I was still working and going to school. Then one night on my way to school it happened again. I got into another wreck in my ex's car! I was on 225 heading to 610 to Katy where my school was, I was on the phone with my mom, ear piece people don't freak out, but I couldn't hear her so I again reached down to turn the radio off and I rear ended the car in front of me.

Yep. That's right folks, if you haven't figured it out yet I'm a stinky driver! So now I had to let Jeremy drive my van and I drove my scooter. Took the kids to school every day one at a time, went to work, the store, everywhere on my little scooter except for school at night I would use the van because the scooter couldn't go far or on freeways I would get ran over. So now that I couldn't go back and forth to my cousin's house that lived 20mins away, I had to move back in with the ex. Heehaw here we go again. Back to square one with the ex. We were starting over, and I was all in this time.

So a few months go by, and Easter was coming up. When one of my best friends Ginny, asked me if the kids and I would like to come to her church for Easter Sunday. I said sure. Because we had both been looking for a church to attend for a while and just couldn't find a good fit. Too many churches we tried gave us both bad vibes, were too big or too small, some we just didn't feel anything, some we attended and not one person would speak to us, and others were full of hypocrites. It's hard to find a good church these days with actual good Christian people in it that are there because they love and worship god and not just there for a social hour. Anyways, so that Sunday she came and picked the kids and me up.

I was nervous because she kept telling me all these amazing things about this church that I have drove by every day for my whole life and never stepped into. When you look at it, from the outside it doesn't seem like much, it's just a regular church and a daycare. Nothing special and I had never heard anything about it so I never went. So we pull up and we all got out of her car. The kids were excited, I'm over here about to puke because my nerves were making me sick, yes I was sober but I didn't think god wanted me anymore because of all the sins I had made, things I had done, and the path I went down. I guess I was ashamed of myself and my past. Well it was too late! I had to go in. We walked in and a man opened the door for us and he was smiling and says hello welcome to Calvary chapel, then a woman smiled said hello were happy to have you here this morning and hugged me and the kids and handed me a flyer.

Then we followed Ginny into the chapel, it was beautiful nothing fancy but it had a sweet presence to it, it was full of pews, white walls with a wooden accent around the room, a small pull pit in the front of the pews and a wooden cross above the pull pit. It was just perfect not all over the top full of gaudy over rated blingy fancy pants church, nope it was a normal perfect little church just as they should be, it's sole purpose was created for the lord and to worship him. I was in awe over this little church. It didn't look anything like the outside. It felt warm, and loving, and so far the people were all super nice. And this woman took us to the second row on the left behind the pastors were Ginny usually sat. Wow Ginny thanks you know I like sitting in the back and not only are we up front but behind the pastors girl, you better know I love you!

Anyways, the worship team started playing their music, and it was cool and hip, and I wasn't use to it but I was digging it, then this guy with a Mohawk started singing. I tell you what, it was like hearing music from heaven, and I was hearing music straight from the lips of an angel. I have heard many of many bands sing onstage but this worship team was truly amazing and they had a powerful anointing especially the guy with the Mohawk, I couldn't help but just stare at him I was in a state of awe now. I'm sure he thought I was a total weirdo just staring at him, mouth all open in and I was in a daze, I couldn't breathe, I couldn't move, I just stood there and starred at him. It felt like how I felt when I first met my daughter's dad. I couldn't even explain the connection I had just made with this man. God was speaking to me about him and the people here, and me and my future here at this little church and I was like wow. My feelings were very surreal, humbling, and profound. I had never felt so many emotions at one time, good emotions warmth, loves, joy and happiness all at once. I felt the Holy Spirit come over me strong.

Then boom, it clicked, helllooooo this is where I belong! Everyone there was smiling dancing and singing, jumping up and down, just praising the lord. You could feel the lords' presence there strong, this little church was over flowing with the holy spirit, it was an actual real church with people who were there for one reason only, to worship the lord! Wow I have never experienced anything so amazing! I wanted to dance, scream, run, and weep. It felt like my skin was going to jump and run off filled with joy around the church on the inside, but all I could do was stand there and take it all in. Just watching everyone around me smiling and dancing and singing to the lord filled my soul with love and warmth those dark feelings and the emptiness inside all that built up just junk over the years I have had, at that moment it was gone. I didn't feel it anymore and I didn't know why.

The worship team finished up and everyone settled down, because it was on fire up in there! I didn't want it to end, I wanted to jump up and down and run in circles around the church screaming Jesus s alive and here! But I didn't because I still couldn't move, so I sat down with everyone else. The preacher started to speak, and when he did his words hit me hard, he spoke the truth, straight from the bible and from his heart. He was so passionate about the words he preached that his anointing was showing, he had a huge light around him, and behind him I saw an angel's wings, there was an angel walking the pull pit with him. It was standing directly behind him and where he walked it walked, when he turned it turned like it was as if he was his guardian and protector. Its wings were so long and beautiful, I just stared for what felt like forever. I had not seen an angel in a long time, only demons surrounded me since I was a small child and I couldn't even remember what a angel looked like it had been so long. The pastor kept on, and towards the end he said a sinner's prayer, so I said it with him.

Then he asked for anyone who wanted prayers to come up to the front so I jumped up and went! I came up to this sweet lady, and she said hello and I said, ok lady do your thing and pray for me! I think I scared her a little her face kind of just froze and her mouth kind of opened like she didn't know what to say about what I just said, well I honestly didn't know what to say to her either and that's what just popped out. Then she just took back her composure like a boss, placed her hands on me like it was no big thing, so I closed my eyes, and she began to pray for me deeply. Man that lady was good at praying! I was listening to what she had to say and I accepted it! I never had anyone pray for me like that where I could feel it. It was a really deep amazing feeling. I was in love with this little church, the people in it and God for placing me there.

After service people just started walking up to me to say hello, hug my neck and to introduce themselves. People here were so nice and friendly, I loved it! I decided that day I wanted to get baptized there. So I continued going to service every week, and at the end of April got baptized. Let me elaborate on my baptism a bit. I went up at the end of service into a room to change into clothes that could get wet. I came out and was waiting on my turn for the preacher to dunk me in the water, I was kind of scared and nervous but this is what I wanted more than anything! My church friend who I look up to and who mentors me, she is who I call my aunt, because she is like family to me, was up there to taking picture of everyone getting baptized, she told me it will be ok and it helped. Anyways, so I get into the water and pastor says who I am and says what he has to say and ask me if I except Jesus as my Lord and savior into my heart, I say yes then he says ok hold your nose and dunks me backwards into the water. When I came up I felt refreshed, I felt amazing like I could jump up out of the water, I felt so many emotions all at once, and I felt cleansed and whole like whole like a little innocent child again like all my sins and bad things I had done were gone my heart was whole again and I was a new person. I can't really elaborate fully even how I felt but it was like nothing I had ever felt. As I started to get out of the pool I was weeping and all I could say to my church aunt was God is good and Jesus is good and cry and I was crying tears of pure joy. My life had now changed and all I wanted was to serve the lord and I owed it all to this little amazingly awesome church.

Then in May my youngest daughter was saved, and in June both my daughter and son were baptized also. My daughter was baptized in the big church, she was extremely overwhelmed with emotions also, and my son was baptized in children's church, he so filled when he was baptized he literally jumped up out of the water over the pastor's wife hands that was holding his towel out for him and screamed I feel live! He was bouncing with excitement and joy I know he was feeling the same things I had felt. But my oldest had already been saved and baptized at her dad's church that the girls had been going to since they were little.

Thank you, father for this awesome experience and placing me in this little amazing church, and thank you, Ginny for caring so deeply for the kids and me for bringing us here with you. You're an amazing woman of God and I really admire you for being such a good sweet and selfless person and always standing up for what you believe. I love you so much sister. Words cannot describe how happy I am, my eyes fill with tears of joy just thinking about it because I'm overwhelmed with the overflowing feeling of love from the people of the church who have opened up their hearts, lives, homes to us. The church was now family, to my little family and I. Thank you for showing us that God does love and care about every single person, and thank you for loving and caring about my kids and I so much, and never judging me ya'll are the best church family anyone could ask for.

Chapter 13

TRIALS AND TRIBULATIONS

After I started going to church the relationship with my boyfriend and I started to change drastically, again. We started to fight even worse than before. He began to become controlling and possessive and tried to alienate me from my family and friends that he didn't like. He worked now at a real job, first time since I had met him. He had held a job for over a year now. But it made him cocky and he would come home and find anything and everything to fight about. He wouldn't just talk down to me but he had started to talk down to and belittle my daughters also. He was making them feel worthless, unloved, unwanted, & their self-esteem had faded away within months. He made them stay outside for hours on end, said they needed to exorcise, walking laps around the park in our apartments, he was in a boot camp style parenting mode now. He had them kneeling on rice in the corner, he would scream in their faces and call them fat little lazy kids, and whatever else he could think of, we had to walk on eggshells around him. Depression had set in on the girls and I and we were miserable! I still remained sober and watched his drug use escalate worse every day.

I was trying to keep my little family together for the kids, especially my son. He loved us both so much and I didn't want to fail my kids again. I prayed and cried out to God to help me find peace in the situation and help Jeremy find God and sober up so we could move forward with our lives together with our children. I would try even writing prayers and putting them under his pillow, anointing the home, and placing hands on him and praying over him as he slept at night. Nothing I did seemed to help, the devil had a tight grasp on him and he wasn't letting go. Even though the devil had him under his thumb, I had faith that God would help him change. So I continued to ask him to come to church every week, and pray openly at dinner over our food, and even listen to Christian music while I cooked and cleaned. My light was shining around him but he never gave in. All I wanted was my family to stay together and be a happy Christian family. I had faith that could move mountains about this and wasn't giving up.

Until one day I went to the store on my scooter to get stuff for dinner, everything seemed okay that day, except on my way back from the store I heard God say, you don't have to stay, it's okay to move on, I understand the situation you are in, and I will provide for you and take care of you and your children. I was confused. I thought well yes it's been rough but what about not giving up? What about fighting for my family? What about keeping my faith? The kids needs a male figure in their lives don't they? He told me to go home and see. He said it's okay daughter, you are mine and I will protect you, just remember to have faith and stand your ground. He said my plans are in motion now, remember what I showed you the first day you came back to me at church. I was still confused but I remembered all what he showed me and said. So when I returned home, the girls were in there in their room crying and Jeremy was screaming very loudly at them, he was cussing at them, calling them names like whores, sluts, and other ugly things, he told them they would never amount to anything and would have to live off men or become strippers or prostitutes to survive. I went into their room and they were huddled down on the ground holding onto one another for dear life. I looked at him and said that's it, I'm done! You can yell at me, call me names, and cut me down, but you can't treat my little girls like this, they're children! He laughed and said you don't have anywhere to go, what are you going to do? I said I don't care the streets would be better than this!

So that next day while he was at work I packed my stuff and a few close friends of mine came over and helped me move everything to storage except some clothes and a few things we would need. He was right I had nowhere to go, but one of my friends said I could come stay with her in her son's room while he was at his dads, but we had to leave when he returned. So we went over there and stayed, and I continued to work, and went everywhere on my scooter. I was very thankful and appreciative for her for letting my children and me in her home. I know it's hard to take on an extra family like that and I will never forget the kindness she showed to us.

Then my dad's situation caused his company to start to fail and he could no longer afford to have me there. I was scared because I had no clue what was going to happen, I couldn't continue to stay with my friend, and without a job I couldn't afford to get a place to live. I was in a limbo so all I could do is put my faith into God and pray to him and give it all to him, I was not sure what my outcome would be but I had faith God had my kids and I under his wings.

A few days passed and then, I got call from my uncle. He said he had heard about what I was going through and wanted to help. He gave me a $1000 to help get a car and said my mom would throw in some also if needed. Wow I was in shock; this is something I never expected. I cried because I was so humbled and very grateful for this unexpected gift. I went and found a car with the help of my step dad within a few days the kids and I were mobile again!

It was almost time for us to leave my friend's house, so my dad said we could go stay at his beach house in Galveston for a while. Since it was summer that's what we did. Although my step dad had said I could come stay with them awhile, but since my mom had just found out she had breast cancer and was fighting with her own health issues that the kids couldn't come with me. But it was almost August which meant school would be starting again soon. That was another headache because I didn't have any money, a permanent place to live, or any gas to drive them back and forth even to school from Galveston to Pasadena every day.

I was at a crossroads, not sure which way to turn. I didn't want to enroll the kids in Galveston school because that would be a hard transition for them, not knowing anyone plus I didn't have the money for uniforms. So I had to make the hardest decision of my life. I had to let the kids go stay at their dad's houses until I could figure it out, and I went to stay with my mom, so I could be close to them. Words cannot express how sad and upset I was going to have to give my children up. It almost broke me.

I didn't understand why, I was weak, afraid, and scared, it was like a wrecking ball had gone through my life again, closing every door I had been through. I cried myself to sleep every night and still continued to prayed every night and keep my faith in God. I knew in my heart he had a plan and I had to stand still and wait for it to brew. I was unable to buy my children their school supplies, back packs shoes and clothes for school, and their dads couldn't help me, they took them in unexpected, and had no money saved either for this. So my mom helped with some of the kids clothes getting them a few outfits each.

Then a friend of mine from church, called me up and asked if he could stop by he had a surprise for me, I said sure. He shows up and says God has his hand on you, and hands me a check for $300. He said it was from his two friends I had only met once, they felt like God had put it on their hearts to help the kids and me out so they called him up, and brought him a check to give me. Wow, I was totally blown away. Nothing like this had ever happened to me. I cried tears of joy because he was right God did have his hand over me. He was protecting me for being a faithful daughter and doing what he asked even when it tore me apart. I was so humbled, thankful, grateful, and appreciative for this unexpected gift. I used it all on the kids like it was supposed to be used. I have never experienced anything like this. My life had been nothing but dark, bad things always happening. I didn't get anything I didn't earn. The love around me from the people in my life was not a deep sweet real unconditional love like what I had been shown now. I had always seen on the television nice people doing nice things for others but never had it happen to me. I had bought the girls stuff they needed, and my son and I was on the way to get his school supplies.

Then it happened again, I had another wreck. This time I was driving down a back road because of traffic, I came up to a four way street. There was only a stop sign at the cross street, I didn't have a stop sign. Well a man who had his granddaughter in the back seat failed to stop, he actually never slowed down like he didn't even see the stop sign, and bam, he hit me hard. I tried to swerve and avoid it but I still got my front end. I called the cops and they issued him a ticket, and I was able to drive it over to the car shop so they could see if it was fixable. Nope no luck it was totaled another one bites the dust, back to square one, I get a break finally everything's going good then this, I move one step forward to get knocked back down further it had seemed. But at least no one was injured.

Well, I was back driving my scooter for a while, until I could find a new vehicle with the insurance money I received. I did find after a month of searching a nice old dodge truck, it was perfect. It was a red old girl with low mileage and one owner. I still have it! Totally a great deal for the little money I paid for it. I was now trying to find a job back in the plants, so I could work a lot of hours and save up for my own place, but I wasn't having any luck. It was September now, kids were in full swing with school, I'm doing everything I can to help my sick parents, find a job go to church every week, and study the bible and pray, a lot. I'm just trying to keep busy and my mind in a positive place. I was bound and determined to get my kids back with me where they belong as soon as I could.

In this waiting process, the ladies from church had the fall retreat that coming weekend, which some of the ladies had gotten together and paid for me to go with them. So I couldn't say no, plus I was super excited about it. I tell you what these church ladies loved me, they took me under their wings and cared and loved for the kids and I. just loving on us and helping us in any way they could. Thank you so much ladies, for not judging me and taking care the kids and I, ya'll mean the world to us. I have never met such an awesome group of woman in my life, and I am proud to be part of their group and their friend. Well my parents was against me going because I still didn't have a job or money and they thought I should stay home and wait to find work. So I prayed about it, and I knew I had to go, plus my spot was paid for and I didn't want that to go to waste, plus I had heard great things about the trip. So I went, and not 20 minutes after we arrived, then I got a call saying I got the plant job I was trying to get and I start that next week and will go till December. Wow that was a total blessing. It had been 40 days of this wrecking ball that had went through my life and destroyed everything. God told me right then he had cleared out all my junk and sifted through my life and heart to remove everything I didn't need, to get me prepared for the path he had set for me. Wow I felt so thankful and honored. It was hard to go through but I kept my faith and stayed still and strong throughout this time. It was one of the hardest things I think I have done yet.

My blessings were coming one after another I was overwhelmed with happiness from my church family and friends who were there by my side and believing in me. I had never experienced such a strong love from anyone in my life, well except from my grandma. So we settled in, had dinner and went to the Friday night service, it was heart filled people getting baptized in the holy spirit, and falling out all over, just praising him. I really had a good time and enjoyed seeing everything happening around me. Then we went to this hill that had a huge empty cross on it and statues of Jesus and his disciples. As we drove up I could feel God's presence, and I saw the statue of

Jesus, it was tall, and beautiful he was standing and facing forward, holding his fishing net. Well we parked and as I got out of the car Jesus head turned over and looked at me and smiled, I heard him say, I've been waiting on you, I love you and I'm so happy to see you, he said it's your time, then his head turned back to its original position. All I could do was walk over to him, bow down touch his feet and pray. Now I know that we are not to worship idols. That wasn't an idol. That was Jesus reaching out to me through this statue, he was not there permanently. I just prayed, and talked to him, and told him to have his way with me, my life is in your hands. It was something I will never forget and will carry with me always.

Now remember, I was a baby Christian, I hadn't been filled by the holy spirit yet, all I had done was dedicate my life to God an got baptized in water but not baptized in the Holy Spirit yet. Some people wait years before God lets them get the Holy Spirit. Everyone's walk is different and I figured it would take time and when God was ready he would fill me. Anyways, the next morning we got up at breakfast, went to the empty cross, then to the church for the morning service, which was my pastors wife who was speaking, and it was just amazing. She is a true blessing, when she speaks with eloquence and angelic profoundness, she is selfless and kind, she speaks with all her heart, its truth, its positive, its love filled, compassionate but stern when needed. She is a true woman of God. She isn't judgmental or negative towards anyone. She has a light that glows so strong around her that it radiates on to others. She is the light in the dark. I truly admire, love and respect and cherish her. She had faith in me when I didn't, she saw greatness in me when all I felt was darkness, and after I was baptized in water she walked up to me and said she was proud of me. Just those few words, I am proud of you, meant so much because no one had said they were proud of me since I was a child. It's the little things she does for others that truly impact lives beyond belief. Just like all of the other women of my church. They hold a special place in my heart.

Anyways, this was my first time hearing her speak outside of our church, so I was super excited. I could feel the Holy Spirit already as we walked in, the worship team was singing, everyone was already in the spirit praising, singing and dancing. I took my seat as I watched what was happening around me. I started to feel the spirit come over me so I began to sing and dance like I had never before. Then my pastors wife came up to speak, and she spoke words that moved me in a way that I have never felt before, I wanted to jump out of my chair and run and scream praise Jesus, her words were filled with love and truth about God and his children and our place with him, I felt the Holy Spirit speaking to me, and everything she said touched me like she was only speaking to me. As she closed the worship team came back up and began to worship and she asked everyone to stand and pray and praise God, while she finished speaking and praying over people. That was when I really felt it, as I was jumping and dancing and singing I felt overwhelmed with emotions I felt warmth inside and all around me. The ladies I was with gathered around me, laid their hands on me and started praying and to hold me up because they knew what was coming, I was singing and laughing uncontrollably, I felt so amazing, then it happened, it felt like lightning went through me, I would have fallen if I hadn't had everyone around me, I was crying and laughing so hard and at the same time, I was so excited I literally peed a little in my pants.

Then one of my favorite ladies which I consider my church aunt who I absolutely just love and adore, started speaking to me, and looking me in the eyes. She said do you understand me? I said of course I do. She then smiled and replied by saying well you have been speaking in tongues for ten minutes, then she placed her hands on my face and started praying and told me to speak, and I lost control of my mouth, tongue, and started speaking in tongues uncontrollably and a bright light surrounded me and I was overwhelmed with even more emotions love, joy, peace inside of me, happiness, and God's grace I felt all pain and brokenness lift out of me. My heart was totally healed of all the junk I had carried for years, like my soul had been renewed. I was reborn in the spirit. And it was the most humbling profound amazing thing that's ever happened to me.

That's when I heard the Holy Spirit tell me to write my story of my life into a book, that I was to speak it, spread it, with God's word all around the world, and help others who were in need of God, to be the light in the dark, to free people of their bondage, and renew their spirit as I just did for you. The spirit spoke of my children and their paths and what they would be destined to do, and many other things. After I calmed down and was able to sit down, two ladies from other churches I had never met, walked up to me at separate times and said they saw me get filled and said exactly what the holy spirit told me, confirming it not once but twice! Soon after that my church aunt said the same things also. After that night my life changed drastically, I will never be the same person I was and I will continue to learn and grow in my faith as I am now.

I still have my own trials and tribulations as everyone but now I can face them head on walking in my faith knowing that my father God is walking next to me and has my back in every step I take. See even though I went through the darkness and was a shadow girl walking in living for nothing over many years and thought I would have died or totally destroyed my family and my life, God pulled me out of the dark and the shadows I resided in, and brought me into the light, and placed me right where I belong again and on the path he had originally placed for me from birth. Psalms 23.4 even though I walk through the darkest valley, I will fear no evil, for you are with me, your rod and staff, they comfort me.

See no matter where you are or what you are going through, there is hope still and people out there who really do care about you. You just have to have faith and seek God through your prayers and get in a good bible based church where you can be guided in your transition from the darkness into the light. It breaks Gods heart to see us suffer or go through rough times, and he wants to see us all become prosperous and live a happy good life, and wants us all to walk with him daily and lean on him and not the world, and be the salt and light of the world to those in the dark still. That's why he gave up his only son who died on the cross for our sins, so we can be forgiven for the things we do and be able to go to heaven with him one day.

Life is hard; the devil will get a hold of you through the world and not let you like he did me. John 3:16 God so loved the world that he gave his one and only son, that whoever believes in him shall not perish, but have eternal life. We can't just be given salvation; we are saved through Gods grace whenever we have faith in his son Jesus. All you have to do is have faith the size of a mustard seed and believe that Jesus died for your sins, then ask him for forgiveness, turn from your sins and repent them. Jesus knows who you are and he loves you so dearly, he knows what's in your heart and he even knows you so well that he knows every hair on your head. So just give your whole self to him and pray for him to forgive you of your sins.

A sinner's prayer

Dear lord, I know I am a sinner and I have sinned, I believe that you died for my sins and rose from the dead. I trust you and fallow you as my lord and savior, I except you to come into my heart and wipe me clean of all the junk built p inside of me, and I ask for your forgiveness of my sins. Father please guide me in my life and help me to do you will.

In your name I pray, Amen.

If you prayed this prayer you just accepted Jesus into your heart

I pray all those who have just read this book will be delivered from all bondages and chains will be broken, I pray Jesus gives them the power and strength to get through the hard times that are upon them, and I pray God removes all the built up junk and lift them out all of the brokenness, that he lifts the depression and oppression from above their heads and cleanses there mind body and souls give them hope and faith father. Father put a hedge of protection around your children and guide them out of the dark and into your arms. Show them there is more to life then what's in the world father. I pray that they take action now and not wait. In Jesus name Amen.

God bless you all.

Jeremiah 29:12-14

Then you will call on me and come and pray to me, and I will listen to you. You will seek me and find me when you seek me with all your heart. I will be found by you," declares the LORD, and will bring you back from captivity. I will gather you from all the nations and places where I have banished you," declares the LORD, "and will bring you back to the place from which I carried you into exile."

M. R. Faith came from a broken home in the suburbs of Pasadena, Texas. She underwent an extremely dark traumatizing childhood which caused her to rebel and drop out of school by 9th grade. She worked for her father's family businesses throughout her life, entertainment industry in management, while attending San Jacinto College. She was married and divorced by 23, with two daughters. Later, to meet another man and having a her son, she started working in the petrochemical plants, and went back to school perusing a bachelor's degree in Psychology at University of Phoenix, but yet again stumbled upon one heart breaking hard time after another putting her life on hold. During this time she became a Christian, dedicated her life to Jesus, and her church, as she found her path with God, she became certified in Construction site Safety Technician and supervisor and wrote her book to help others in their life trials.

Behindtheeyesofashadowgirl@yahoo.com

Printed in the United States
By Bookmasters